What leaders ar
The Simple-Min

"I have worked with

past 20 years, and have watched his model evolve through practice and success. This insightful book provides the tools and philosophy to help us all cope with our increasingly complicated professional and personal lives."

Lance J. Bronnenkant, PhD. President & CEO, FEI Enterprises, Ltd.

"Dr. Greenslade led us to levels of growth and productivity previously unachievable by our organization. His strategic vision, management skills and solid scientific background were invaluable tools for us. His book reveals these tools."

Pouru Bhiwandiwala, MD, Chair, Ipas Board of Directors

"Everyone serious about their careers, no matter how competent or experienced, will benefit from *The Simple-Minded Manager.* Each of us needs to learn, or re-learn, to be simple-minded"

John Vacek, Executive Search Specialist

"Dr. Greenslade understands that healthy organizations are simply healthy individuals bound together by common vision"

Robert Ferguson, Ph.D., Clinical Psychologist / Executive Coach

"Dr. Greenslade guided the worldwide introduction of important health care technologies. His management strategies work"

Dr. George Brown, VP, The Population Council

"Important guidance on leadership strategies for more effective teams in today's changing work environments"

Joanne Spicehandler, Organization Development Consultant

"Able scientist brings Aristotelian process to business practice"

Nestor G. Anderson, President, Anderson and Collins.

"Solid advice for entrepreneurs and established businesses"

Norman George, Partner, Bridge Associates International

"Dr. Greenslade's management tools work"

Denise Resnik, Pharmaceutical Consultant

"Particularly important for young growing professionals"

Susan Allen, M.D., Physician, Manager and Regulatory Authority

"Pragmatic guidance crisply communicated"

Peter Knudsen, Novelist, Television and Radio Producer, District 37 Governor, Toastmasters International

"Tools for developing satisfying careers and healthy institutions"

Jill Sheffield, CEO, Family Care International

"Simple memorable lessons, beautifully delivered"

Anna Holland, President & CEO, Durapave

"Good management, good business, good reading"

Candi Copas, Vice President, Networking Enterprises

The *Simple-Minded Manager* presents a clear pathway to start managing a group of individuals without changing your own personality, and it's amazingly simple!

Alan Schwartz, PhD, MBA, Director, Business Development, Karolinska Innovations AB, Stockholm, Sweden

The SIMPLE-MINDED Manager

Cutting Through Your Work-Life Chaos

Forrest C. Greenslade, PhD

Design: Kathryn E. Greenslade

Illustrations: Kristin Needham

Intercare21st Publishing, Chapel Hill, North Carolina

THE SIMPLE-MINDED MANAGER
Cutting Through Your Work-Life Chaos
By Forrest C. Greenslade, Ph.D.

Published by Intercare21st Publishing
Chapel Hill, North Carolina
Kate Armstrong, Publisher

The Simple-Minded Manager / by Forrest C. Greenslade, Ph.D.
First Edition

Design by Kathryn E. Greenslade
Illustration by Kristin Needham

Visit us online at http://www.intercare21st.com

Publishers Cataloging-in-Publication

Greenslade, Forrest C., 1939-
The simple-minded manager : cutting through your work-life chaos / Forrest C. Greenslade , illustrations and design: Kathryn E, Greenslade
--1st ed.
LCCN: 00-190258
ISBN: 0-9678770-08

1. Business communications. 2. Managemnet.
3. Leadership. 4. Organizational change.
I. Greenslade, Kathryn. II. Title.
HF5718.G74 2000 658.4'5
QBI00-900476

Library of Congress Card Number: 00-190258

This book is dedicated to my friends and colleagues of the Bull City Toastmasters Club in Durham, North Carolina. They provided a laboratory for testing these essays. They bolstered my spirits when I needed support, and challenged me to communicate more effectively when I needed objective evaluation.

A better group of people you will not find.

TABLE OF CONTENTS

About The Author

Forrest C. Greenslade, Ph.D. is a scientist, manager, writer and speaker who has learned a lot about growing productive careers and decisive organizations. He loves to share what he has learned. Dr. Greenslade has held leadership positions in some of the world's most important biomedical organizations including, the Population Council, Pfizer and Johnson & Johnson. Most recently he was President of Ipas. He has also served as Industry Liaison Representative to a USFDA advisory panel.

Greenslade founded Intercare in 1982.

A perpetual student, Greenslade attended numerous management courses after he completed graduate school and a post-doctoral fellowship. Later, he participated in the Center For Creative Leadership "Leadership at the Peak" program. An active member of Toastmasters International, he has earned Advanced Toastmaster Gold and Competent Leader Awards. He is a member of the National Speakers Association.

Dr. Greenslade has authored more than 140 books, book chapters, papers, and webarticles. His straightforward writings and speeches on Simple-Minded Management provide men and women, and the organizations in which they work, with practical strategies for satisfying professions and healthy institutions.

Acknowledgement

I am indebted to Dr. Chandra Louise for her substantive guidance and editorial advice.

Disclaimer

This book is designed to provide information and to stimulate thinking about personal, professional and organizational growth. It is sold with the understanding that the publisher and author are not engaged in rendering legal or other professional services. The purpose of this collection of essays is to educate and entertain. This is not a scholarly work. Quite the contrary, it is simply meant to communicate the management lessons learned by the author. The author, publisher and Intercare21st Publishing shall have neither liability nor responsibility to any person or entity with respect to any loss or damage caused, or alleged to be caused, directly or indirectly by the information in this book.

If you do not wish to be bound by the above, you may return this book to the publisher for a full refund.

Frustra
fit per plura,
quod fieri potest
per pauciora

Is it possible for people to have productive professions and satisfying lives?

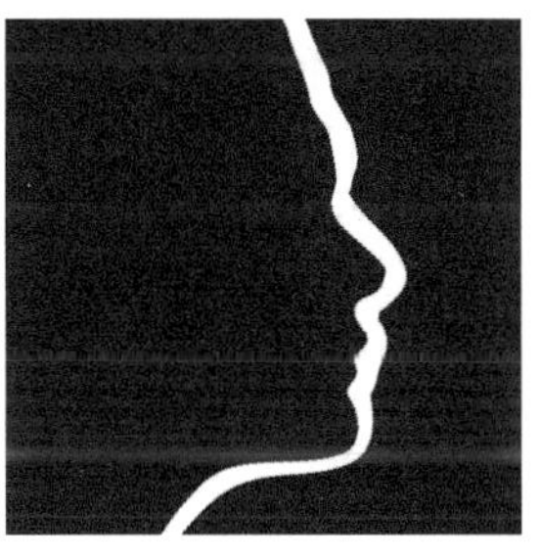

WILLIAM:

cutting through the chaos

I remember a discussion I had many years ago with a supervisor. He was telling me how hard he worked, and how much he needed a break. I countered by telling him how hard I was working. Surely, I worked harder and was more stressed than he. We went back and forth, each growing more red-faced. Then suddenly, I stopped. Why was I competing with my boss? Why was I entering this contest, trying to determine who worked harder? Why had I fallen into the all-too-common trap of thinking that my value as a person rested on how hard I worked or how stressed I felt?

We live in challenging times. We feel that we face issues that people have never faced before. We have longer working lives. We work in a global, interconnected, complicated economy. Technology is changing the way we work everyday. We perceive less job security and a more frenetic way of life. We are caught in the shuffle of being better, faster, and cheaper than the competition. How often we hear the lament, "I don't know how long I can keep up this pace." "I can't keep up with all the technology." "There's too much to read and too much to do." Frustration is running high. Satisfaction is rare.

Decisions must be made at the speed of light. But what goes on between the ears is the same as ever before. Human nature hasn't changed at all. Yet as times change, management and organization development theories become more complex. No one has the time to frame simple, fundamental ideas that bring order to our complex lives.

Sometimes it all seems so chaotic.

Well, a young man named William found the solution to all this.

William was born in a little town near London. He entered into the Franciscan Order at an early age. His schooling concentrated on the study of math and logic. Later, William took a traditional course of studies at Oxford University, and began to write and lecture on his ideas. Unfortunately, William's opinions so offended the faculty at Oxford that he left the University without completing his Masters Degree. William then pursued his academic career in France, where he again challenged the authority of those who dogmatically held to complex and confusing organizational theories. It was there that William articulated a simple idea that cut through all the confusion.

I should tell you that William was born in the year 1285. The little town near London was called Ockham. What William of Ockham challenged were the complex theological "truths" of the day. William of Ockham's simple idea profoundly changed the way we think about human kind and its place in the world. The "Gurus" of the day were tied to complex theological constructs that had built up over hundreds of years. The new ideas and technologies from scientific inquiry were colliding directly with the old accepted premises. Complex, and to William, illogical explanations were framed by theologians to reconcile new and old understandings of the world.

William of Ockham cut through all of this complexity with one simple phrase:

Frustra fit per plura,

quod fieri potest per pauciora

A rough translation of his idea is,

"the simplest of theories is preferable"

or

"the simpler the explanation,

the closer to the truth."

William used this simple logic so effectively to cut through the confusing theories of the day, the idea became known as "Ockham's Razor"

Well, we face the same problems today. New ideas, technologies and human relationships are colliding with long-accepted organizational "truths." Managerial and organization development theorists propagate increasingly complex constructs about us, and our institutions. Most of us yearn for a few fundamental ideas to help simplify our chaotic lives.

A New Edge on Ockham's Razor

"Ockham's Razor" is as valid today as it was in the 14th Century. The idea that "the simpler the explanation the closer to the truth" can be a powerful tool in forging order from the chaos that typifies our frenetic work-lives. Perhaps a 21st Century update of William's theorum should be called "Ockham's Lazer", a tool to cut through unneeded complexity and expose simple truths.

Is it possible to simplify our lives? Can we achieve that balance in life, that holistic center, that each of us seeks on some level, and still achieve professional success?

I think so,

and "Ockham's Lazer"

is a good start.

Finding simple explanations and bringing about simple solutions to today's apparently complex organizational problems requires each of us to be more simple-minded.

IT IS OFTEN DIFFICULT TO BE SIMPLE-MINDED.

The Simple-Minded Manager views problems in a certain way. While recognizing that situations are complex, the Simple-Minded Manager understands that there is usually a simple pure component, composed of only one thing that can be isolated and altered— a simple matter.

The Simple-Minded Manager concentrates on solutions that are:

Occurring or considered alone	— **the simple truth**
Not involved or complicated	— **a simple task**
Without additions or alterations	— **a simple yes or no**
With little or no ornamentation or embellishment	— **a simple message**
Not elaborate, elegant or luxurious	— **plain talk**

The Simple-Minded Manager interacts with others in ways that are:

Unassuming or unpretentious	— **not affected**
Not guileful or deceitful	— **sincere**

The Simple-Minded Manager is unconcerned if this style is misinterpreted as:

Manifesting little sense or intelligence	**— a simple way of thinking**
Humble, ordinary or common	**— simple and folksy**
Unworldly or unsophisticated	**— naíve**

The Simple-Minded Manager is more interested in accomplishment than appearance.

Is it possible to grow organizations that don't force people to choose between having productive professions and satisfying lives? I know that it is, and that is why I have written this collection of essays. They are lessons that I have learned, and tools that I have discovered over a long career in commercial, governmental and non-profit organizations. I want to share these simple, and hopefully memorable, lessons and tools with future leaders.

I know that it is possible to grow decisive organizations that respect the right, need, and ability of workers to be satisfied people, good parents and have productive careers. In fact, if we are to be a truly productive society, it will be the responsibility of tomorrow's leaders to do so. I emphatically believe that this is primarily an individual responsibility and an individual opportunity. It is up to each of us to ensure that our personal and professional lives move in the directions that we want. We cannot wait for organizations to change — each of us has the power to profoundly influence the cultures of the institutions in which we work.

We are in control! We do have choices!

Only a Simple-Minded Manager can cut through the chaos.

People accomplish the most when their self-interests are being served.

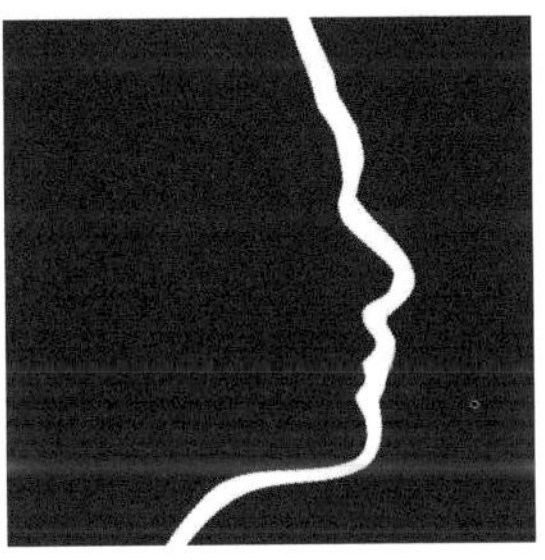

DANIEL & CHARLOTTE:

people are selfish—a simple-minded premise

Daniel is the CEO of a rapidly growing consulting company. He founded it. It was his vision and hard work that made it an unprecedented success. He has a bold strategy for continued growth and success.

But Daniel is a troubled man. He is troubled by the attitudes of his professional employees. "They don't have the drive that I did when I was their age," he thinks. "They aren't willing to sacrifice for the company like I did." Daniel doesn't understand why his employees aren't dedicated to the future of the organization.

Charlotte is a young project manager in the company, and if Daniel would only ask her, she could tell him why. Charlotte is "maxed out" by the ever-increasing demands to complete more and more projects

Daniel doesn't understand why his employees aren't dedicated to the future of the organization.

in ever decreasing time frames. Whenever she gets one project done there are several more projects, all behind schedule, waiting for her to start. She can't maintain this pace much longer. Her fatigue is mounting and her irritability is increasing. Charlotte's life is in chaos!

Charlotte is frustrated. As a professional employee who is exempt from some provisions of the Fair Labor Standards Act, she gets no extra pay for completing more projects or for working longer hours. Instead, her own professionalism and desire to succeed motivate her. Charlotte naturally takes great pride in her work. However, in this situation, she doesn't have enough time to do a decent job, let alone meet her own professional standards. The pressures of the job have usurped Charlotte's pride. She only feels inadequate and unable to do satisfactory work.

Where is Charlotte's reward? If she produces superior work, she is rewarded with more work. She cannot remember the last time her supervisor said, "thanks, that was a great job." Charlotte doesn't see that she is sharing in the success of the company. She isn't!

Charlotte is frustrated. She gets no extra pay for completing more projects or for working longer hours.

Daniel has forgotten a simple fact. His employees are not working to make him rich or his company successful. They are working for themselves. They are working for their own self-interests, goals and dreams.

Daniel, in pursuing his dream, has lost sight of a simple truth — People are selfish. Daniel has forgotten that people do not work to serve organizations; people work to serve themselves. In doing so, he has created an environment that is thwarting the dreams of his employees.

And this is the fundamental premise of this book — People are selfish. They are motivated by their own self-interests. People simply accomplish the most when their self-interests are being served. The most productive organizations are those in which the interests of individuals are best aligned with the interest of the whole.

The core message of the Simple-Minded Manager is this.

If you are a manager, or strive to be one, you must recognize that the key to your success is matching your self-interests with those of others.

Whether you strive to manage a Fortune 500 corporation or just your own life, understanding that people are selfish empowers you to grow both satisfying careers and decisive organizations.

So, which way ought each of us to go?

BE YOUR OWN MISSIONARY:

where you want to go

"Would you tell me please which way I ought to go from here?" said Alice.

"That depends a good deal on where you want to go," said the cat.

"I don't care much where," said Alice.

"Then it doesn't matter which way you go," said the cat.

From Lewis Carroll's Alice's Adventures in Wonderland, 1865

Very few organizational leaders are like Lewis Carroll's Alice, not caring much which way they are going themselves or the direction they are steering the organizations they lead. However, they may well appear not to care by their actions. We live and work in chaotic times. Personal and professional decision-making in such times requires seemingly contradictory premises: dogged adherence to continuous management process and openness to complex changes in the environments in which we function. Factors inside and outside our institutions produce cross-valent winds that buffet us in many directions every day.

Growing more decisive management structures is the most daunting task facing leaders at all levels of governmental, civil and commercial organizations. Growing productive and satisfying life-scripts for ourselves in the contexts of these institutions is an essential goal for most people, a goal that each of us can achieve.

I use the word "growing" purposefully. Agrarian metaphors like "nurturing" and "shepherding" more accurately describe the strategic decision-making process than "constructing" and "building" architectural images or "manufacturing" and "assembling" industrial icons that are usually used.

So, which way ought each of us to go?

Well, our friend the Cheshire Cat is right. That depends a great deal on where each of us wants to go. It depends a great deal on our own individual sense of mission.

What do we mean when we speak of mission?

The word is rich and complex. Here are some of the connotations:

- A body of persons sent to conduct negotiations or establish relations with a foreign country
- The business with which such a body of persons is charged
- A permanent diplomatic office abroad
- A body of persons sent to a foreign land by a religious organization—to spread its faith or provide educational, medical, and other assistance

- A mission established abroad
- A body of experts or dignitaries sent to a foreign country
- The district assigned to a mission worker
- A building or compound housing a mission
- An organization for carrying on missionary work in a territory
- A series of special-services for purposes of proselytizing
- A welfare or educational organization established for the needy people of a district
- A special assignment given to a person or group: an agent on a secret mission
- A combat operation assigned to a person or military unit
- An aerospace operation intended to carry out specific program objectives: a mission to Mars
- An inner calling to pursue an activity or perform a service; a vocation

The word "**mission**" has all the inferences of: assignment, task, charge, purpose, sortie, duty, commission, goal, objective, calling, aim, lifework, and vocation. In our context, we usually speak of the mission of an organization, but it can also be applied to individual growth. But which way ought we each to grow. To paraphrase our friend the Cheshire Cat, that depends a great deal on how each of us wants to grow. Knowing how to grow depends on an individual sense of mission. To achieve maximal professional growth requires each person to become a missionary. I ask each of you to become your own missionary: to articulate your inner calling; to define your specific objectives; to achieve your compelling goal.

I ask each of you to become your own evangelist, apostle, teacher, pastor, herald, messenger and propagandist.

A friend tells a story about a Quaker missionary who was riding his mule thorough the mountainous Sierra Madre country of Mexico, and the mule was being obstinate. It balked often, threw the missionary off repeatedly, and bit him at every possible opportunity. The missionary, being of the Society of Friends, was unable to raise his hand against either man or beast, and put up with the mule's recalcitrant behavior with saint-like equanimity. One day, however, when the mule had been particularly obstinate, bitten the missionary twice, and threw him down a small precipice, he lost patience. "Friend mule", he said, "thou knowest that I am a man of faith, of the Society of Friends, and cannot strike thee. Thou also knowest that thy behavior has been beyond human forbearance." "But what thou does not know is that presently I shall sell thee to a Methodist, who will then proceed to beat the living tar out of thee!!!!"

Now this Quaker missionary is like most of us, striving to achieve a goal, while trying to live up to strongly-held values, and working under irritating and obstructive conditions. To become your own missionary you need to understand and articulate what links your goals and your values. If you do, even the most irritating and obstructive conditions will not deter you from pursuing your mission and accomplishing your long-term goals.

It is not that difficult! If you will ask and honestly answer four straightforward questions, and make most decisions according to the answers, I guarantee you a more productive and fulfilling professional and personal life. Here they are:

1. **Who am I** — How do you define yourself personally and professionally?

2. **What do I believe** — What priority values guide your career course?

3. **What do I do** — What is your primary professional goal?

4. **How do I do it** — What unique approach do you use to reach that goal?

Here is the hard part — each of these questions must be answered in approximately seven words. Taken together these concise answers are your own Professional Mission Statement.

- Write it down.
- Carry it with you.
- Share it with your family, friends and colleagues.
- Most important, use your Mission Statement as your critical decision-making tool.

When you are framing long- or short- term plans, ask yourself, "Does this strategy most effectively pursue my mission?" When deciding on an educational or career opportunity, ask yourself, "Is this choice the most consistent with my mission?" In setting priorities for daily activities, ask yourself, "Which of these alternative activities will most productively advance my mission?" When dealing with personal issues, ask yourself, "Are my personal and professional goals consistent and integrated components of my overall mission?"

My Personal and Professional Mission:

Who I am

____

____

____

____

What I believe

____

____

____

____

What I do

____

____

____

____

How I do it

____

____

____

____

Of course, articulating your own Professional Mission Statement is only one step in your decision-making strategy. Linking it to your own values system is essential. Long-term planning is key. But you can't plan your journey without understanding your own personal and professional destination. So, don't be like Alice. Know where you are going, understand your own mission, and

— most important

— be you own missionary.

What's it worth
to me?

WHAT'S IT WORTH TO YOU?

your work-life values hierarchy

One day Kelly, a key member of our company's executive team, came into my office. She was obviously agitated. She asserted her disapproval of my interactions with a young project manager. Kelly felt that I had not provided this young man with adequate guidance, "Forrest, you let him just twist in the wind." As we discussed the issue further, it became clear to both Kelly and me that we had quite different values related to supervision. Interestingly, we both used the same word to describe our approach to supervision — we both believed in "nurturing" employees. Kelly valued protecting employees from discomfort, confusion and anxiety. I valued protecting employee's autonomy and opportunity to solve problems on their own.

Of course, we were both right!

Over the next several weeks, Kelly and I had a number of similar discussions. We came to understand that, while we shared the same mission goals and objectives for the organization, we had rather different personal and professional values systems. We learned to better understand the values contexts of each other's language. We gained more respect for each other's approaches, because we were more aware of the values that underpinned them.

I began to appreciate the powerful influence that people's work-life values have on the way they make decisions. I began to comprehend how the values hierarchies of the individuals on the leadership team must be considered in framing the operating principles and strategic plan of the organization. I came to understand that, if I didn't pay attention to the values hierarchies of the entire staff, it would be virtually impossible to gain sufficient consensus for executing the plan.

On the next page is a simple tool that I found very useful.

You can use it to define your work-life values hierarchy. There are 25 values that most people hold as important.

Write down each of these values on separate scraps of paper, or enter them into your computer. Now, arrange them in order of their importance to you. Place the most important at the top and order them to the least important at the bottom. This is your own work-life values hierarchy. Write it down on page 22. Carry it with you. Use it, along with your personal-professional mission statement, as a decision-making tool.

Feel comfortable to share your values hierarchy with friends and colleagues. This helps the people who are most important to you to better understand what is most important to you.

25 Personal/Professional Values

Financial Security

Acquisition of Wealth

Stability and Order

Power and Authority

Good Health, Safety and Comfort

Independence, Autonomy

Peace of Mind

Gaining Knowledge

Having Close Friends

Mastering Skills

Pleasure, Relaxation and Leisure

Professional Growth

Self Fulfillment

Self Esteem, Self Respect

Personal Growth

Prestige, Status, Respect from Others

Adventure, Excitement

Accomplishment, Achievement of Goals

Change, New Experiences

Doing Something Important

Making Acquaintances

Spirituality

Responsibility

Helping Others, Improving Society

Family Responsibilities

My Work/Life Values Hierarchy:

1 ____________________

2 ____________________

3 ____________________

4 ____________________

5 ____________________

6 ____________________

7 ____________________

8 ____________________

9 ____________________

10 ____________________

11 ____________________

12 ____________________

13 ____________________

14 ____________________

15 ____________________

16 ____________________

17 ____________________

18 ____________________

19 ____________________

20 ____________________

21 ____________________

22 ____________________

23 ____________________

24 ____________________

25 ____________________

Keep this tool handy and use every day. For each important decision that you must make, ask yourself

— What's it worth to me?

Many time-management tools actually prevent us from managing truly important issues.

Time's Fun When You're Havin' **FLIES**:

invest your time wisely

They say, "Time flies when you are having fun." Actually, time flies even when you are not having so much fun. Most people that I know tell me that finding time for the "important things" is their most pressing management problem. It must be true. An entire industry has developed around time management. You can spend from hundreds to thousands of dollars on calendars, planners, organizers, software, hardware, seminars and courses to manage your time. These are all useful tools for controlling the myriad of demands on every minute of every day.

However, these same tools may actually make your real management problem even worse! I am convinced that for most people the real management problem is investing enough critical time in dealing with the fundamental long-term issues that we face in our organizations and lives. Most time management tools concentrate so much on shuffling every minute of every day to accommodate the thousands of meetings, memos, and reports addressing short-term priorities that they actually prevent us from managing truly important long-term issues.

Don't get me wrong! I like such tools. I use them. They are useful. However, they are only useful as aids in accomplishing meaningful long-term time management. So, I offer a gentle reminder to help you get your time really under control.

Time's fun when you're havin' FLIES.

Focus on very few long-term goals.

Based on your own organizational and personal mission statements (see page 16), identify three to five long-term critical goals. Write them down on page 28. Make them simple, clear and measurable. Envision a three- to five-year time frame for accomplishing the goals.

Openly share these goals with your supervisor, colleagues, family and other stakeholders in you and your organization. Many times, their "buy-in" will make the difference in your ultimate success in pursuing and completing these objectives.

Lay out your own detailed strategic plan to accomplish these goals.

This requires working backward from the goals to identify key steps and dependencies that must be managed (see workbook on page 28 and be sure to commit this step to paper, too). There are plenty of planning tools to help you with this process. The important step is to invest your time in this personal long-term planning.

Again, make your plan known to those people close to you so they understand what you plan to do and why. How are you (and they) going to know what is most important in the short-term if you are not clear about your intentions for the long-term.

Implement your plan immediately.

This is critical. Don't let today's priority or this morning's crisis keep you from initiating your long-term strategy. If you don't implement immediately, the chaos of day after day will squander your time, preventing real long-term accomplishment. Write down the first, immediate steps that you take on page 28.Don't forget to mark down the date. Check back in a month. If you need to reinitiate! Don't let yourself lose momentum over time.

Evaluate your progress every day.

Each day, hold yourself accountable to your mission, goals and strategic plan. No one else will! You've written it down. Now make sure you check it every day for a progress report. Be objective. Be critical. In the hustle and hassle of each hectic day, ask yourself,

"What have I done today

to execute my strategy?"

This will help you set better priorities for the many other demands on your time.

Stay on course.

...No matter what immediate priorities appear to be important. I'm not advocating rigidity. Obviously, your plan must adjust to your progress and to environmental changes. However, we live in chaotic times, and many short-term challenges appear more important when viewed with short-time vision than they are when understood with long-time insight. So keep your long-term goals and strategies always in view.

The pace of life and business is increasingly hectic. It is increasingly more difficult to deal with the daily demands on our time. It is increasingly more challenging to recognize that time is our most important human resource.

So, Remember ... **Time's fun when you're havin' FLIES.**

F **ocus** on the long-term.

Identify three to five long-term critical goals.

1 ______________________________

2 ______________________________

3 ______________________________

4 ______________________________

5 ______________________________

L **ay out** your own strategic plan.

Identify key steps and dependencies that must be managed.

1 ______________________________

2 ______________________________

3 ____

____

4 ____

____

5 ____

____

I **mplement** it immediately.

What is the first step that I took? Date ________________

____

E **valuate** your progress each day.

What did I do today? Date ________________________

____

What did I do today? Date ________________________

____

What did I do today? Date ________________________

____

S **tay** on course.

Invest your time wisely. It is YOUR time!

Grab and hold on to something just beyond your reach.

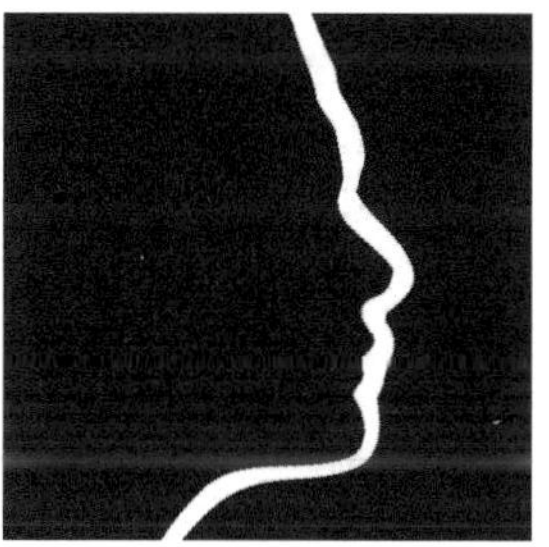

ROBIN:

seize the DAY

Sometimes lessons come to you unexpectedly. The other day I rented an old movie — The Dead Poets Society, starring Robin Williams. Williams' character is a teacher in a rigid private school. He attempts to inspire the young boys in his class to break out from their programmed thinking to sense a passion for creativity. In a way it is a tragic story, because the school authorities, considering his style too disruptive to their tradition, ultimately force the teacher to leave. In a way it is a triumphant story, because in that act, the authorities spark defiance in several students that ignites the very passions the teacher so passionately advocates. The teacher's simple lesson that evokes these explosive actions and reactions is Carpe Diem — Seize the Day.

For most of us in these chaotic times, seizing any day feels impossible. There are so many forces buffeting us about. But it is essential!

You will not get this day back! Your Vision, Mission and Strategic Plan correctly focus on your future. Your values are legacies of your past. What links them is simply this day.

So, seize the DAY.

Seize the Decisiveness that is within you today. Make the choices that pursue your mission now, the judgements that manifest your values now, the resolution that executes your plan now. Have the will to follow your own path now.

Seize the Attainable that documents your progress. Employ resources that are accessible today. Use strategies that are approachable now. Identify short-term goals, consistent with your mission, that are obtainable in the present. Concentrate on what is possible today. But, most important—

Seize the Yearning. Grab and hold on to that persistent longing for something just beyond your reach.

Seize the DAY.

People
are not afraid to buy.
They are afraid of
being sold.

DOING **DEALS**:

selling your most important product

Lets start out with a small survey. How many of you want to be failures—poor— victims? Not many positive responses are there? It's obvious isn't it? No one actively seeks these goals! No, we all want success, financial health, and personal control over our own lives. Well, I am going to give you a sales strategy that will absolutely guarantee you success, financial security and personal autonomy. I will also offer you a product to sell that will bring you profit beyond your wildest dreams.

Selling is not that difficult! Think about it. People want products and services that solve their problems. Your task as a sales person is simply to cause a potential customer to recognize the value of what you are selling. You need to facilitate the process by demonstrating your respect for the product. You have to "halo" the product in pleasant associations for the prospective customer.

Experts will tell you that there are five steps in selling*:

1. **Find out your potential customer's needs.** Turn your conversations with him or her into interviews in which you seek information and discover what you can do for that person or group.

2. **Gain that person's confidence.** People buy products and services because they feel that the sales person understands them. Listen to understand their thoughts and feelings.

3. **Sell a solution.** Effective selling is never a conflict. You must help people make mature decisions and take actions that are truly in their own interests. Take a positive problem-solving approach.

4. **Anticipate objections.** Most objections are actually unanswered questions. Help your potential customer discover what question he or she is asking. Guide and respond. Don't argue or push.

5. **Make the close.** Your entire sales presentation is part of your close. You are done only when your potential customer fully understands the savings involved or the benefits that he or she will receive from the product or service.

Now, here is my sure-fire selling technique. I call it Doing DEALS. I use this phrase to describe a selling process — Doing DEALS by selling solutions. People buy solutions to their problems. People are not afraid to buy. They are afraid of being sold or of making mistakes. So, to sell a product or service you must help people understand how your product or service will solve an important problem for each person.

---

*Adapted in part from: The Sales Training Speech, in The Professional Speaker Manual, Toastmasters International, 1997.

Here is how to Do DEALS by **Selling Solutions.**

Demonstrate
— Show the inherent values of your product or service.

Evaluate
— Collect information on your prospective customer's needs and problems.

Assure
— Communicate your sincere interest in the person.

Listen
— Really understand that person's problem.

Solve
— Close only if your product or service is the best solution to that person's problem.

If you use this selling technique, if you do DEALS, you will increase your probability of success, increase your income and put yourself in the driver's seat.

Now, here is the product that I promised would provide you with success beyond your wildest dreams.

It is you. Yes, you are the only product that will absolutely guarantee your success. You must sell yourself and your ideas every day. I don't mean this in a trivial or cynical way. Selling yourself is the noblest endeavor that you can undertake.

Earlier, I talked about several strategies for personal and organizational growth. I talked about how important it is to be your own missionary — to define: who you are, what you believe, what you do, and how you do it. I stressed the power of values and the question, what's it worth to me? I also said that time's fun when you're havin' FLIES — to Focus on long-term goals, to Lay out a plan, to Implement the plan immediately, to Evaluate your progress each day, and to Stay on course.

Now, I am offering you a tool to use every day in accomplishing all of the above. It is the unbeatable combination of a foolproof selling technique and the best product in the world. I offer you —

Doing DEALS: Selling Yourself.

Demonstrate
— Live your values every day (see page 22).

Evaluate
— Remain objective about your strengths and about areas that you should strengthen.

Assure
— Communicate your values and sincerity to each person with whom you interact.

Listen
— Understand others and their problems.

Solve
— Create solutions for others rather than contributing to their problems.

If you use this selling technique — and if you use it to sell yourself and your ideas, I absolutely, 100 percent, guarantee you more success, financial health and personal control over your life.

So why are you just sitting there —

Go out and start Doing DEALS!

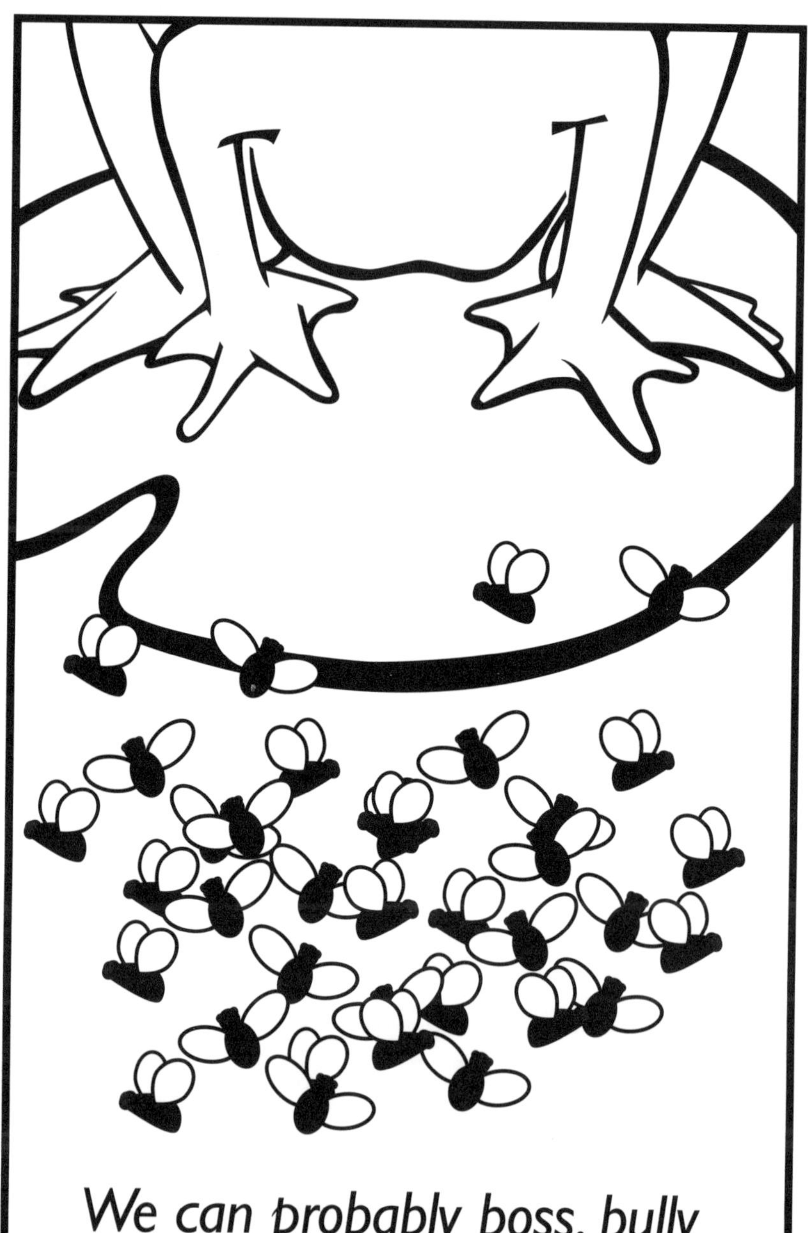

We can probably boss, bully and squeeze employees into productivity for a while…

DON'T BOSS, COACH*:

productive supervision

My colleague Chantal told me about her first experience with a boss. She was a college kid, and she had a summer job cleaning dorm rooms.

"I was enthusiastic about the job—until my supervisor yelled at me about the way I was cleaning the garbage pails. Yes, you heard me right—the garbage pails! Did you know that there was a right versus a wrong way to clean garbage pails????

Neither did I.

It was about power. She loved the fact that she could have power over the students. Here we were, a bunch of Ivy-League students—and we were training to go somewhere. She decided to exert her power where she could, before we became her bosses.

It may have made her feel better, but what did it do for the workplace? I know someone who was so resentful that she managed to figure out how to sleep, all day, on the job! This person would pull out the couches in the student lounge and sleep behind them! Somehow the supervisor never thought to look there.

The rest of us supported our coworker. We helped her to do this. Obviously our attitudes were not too great either."

It is important to remember that the word "boss" has the connotations of "control", "dominate" and "roughen", as well as "supervise."

Chantal also told me about her friend who had worked very hard on a report. Finally, after she was done with her masterpiece, she handed it to her boss.

BAD BOSSING results in poisoned relationships, high turnover, lost productivity and, in many cases, law suits.

After about a week, she still didn't have any feedback, so she asked her boss about the report. He just said, "the report needs work." Well—the "work" that he did was to change one sentence out of a 24-page report. One sentence out of a 24-page report! Would you consider that to be significant work?

Chantal's stories are actually very minor examples of bad bossing that occurs in today's work place. Bad bossing results in poisoned relationships, high turnover, lost productivity and, in many cases, law suits.

When I look back on my own career, I have had a bad boss or two

- **bosses who took credit for my ideas,**
- **bosses who excluded me from the decision-making process,**
- **bosses who paid little attention to my professional development.**

But I also had some excellent supervisors

- **mentors who saw in me qualities that I didn't even know that I possessed,**
- **facilitators who furthered my own and the organization's accomplishment.**

When I look back at my own managerial experience, I must admit to occasions when I failed to catalyze optimal professional growth in people who reported to me, and times when I did this very effectively.

When I think about it, the most productive supervision occurred, whether I was the supervisor or the person being supervised, when neither of us was very bossy. It is important to remember that the word "boss" has the connotations of "control", "dominate" and "roughen", as well as "supervise."

The most productive supervisory relations in my experience were much more like those developed between a professional performer and a coach. These were designed alliances, where we recognized that the real power was in the relationship, rather than in either of the individuals. Such relationships were obviously based on shared understandings of both personal and organizational missions, shared values, and common visions of the future.

While every person in an organization needs to contribute to the most productive supervisory relationships, it is clearly the supervisor's responsibility to initiate them. So, here is some simple advice to supervisors. Don't boss, COACH.

Don't boss — COACH.

Collaborate
— Form associations with people who report to you for common benefit — benefit to you, benefit to them, and benefit to the organization. Together, negotiate goals consistent with personal and organizational missions. Share the outcomes.

Observe
— Continuously monitor their progress. Watch their activities. Examine their approaches. Elicit information from them. Pay attention to the feedback that they provide. Consider their feelings as valuable information. Celebrate their accomplishments.

Ask
— Seek information from them. Invite their participation. Request their input. Require their involvement. Impose responsibility, obligation and accountability.

Challenge
— Engage them in dialog. Dispute their assumptions. Take exception to their answers. Confront their problems. Defy their fears.

Hypothesize
— Formulate theories for them to explore. Apply logic to their assertions. Assert explanations accounting for facts for them to test.

What are the rewards of COACHing?

- When you COACH as a supervisor, you motivate employees to maximize their performance and growth.

- When you **COACH,** you provide employees with the context of their work and the autonomy to accomplish it.

- When you **COACH,** you are demanding of employee accomplishment.

- When you **COACH,** you recognize that their work is their accomplishment, and their accomplishment is your accomplishment.

- When you **COACH,** your employees benefit, you benefit and the organization does, too.

Now, I recognize the pressures that today's competitive environment imposes on today's supervisors. We are all worried about our own jobs. We are pressured to operate with short-term mentalities. We can probably boss, bully and squeeze employees into productivity for a while, and replace them when they are burned out or quit in desperation.

But this is a disastrous strategy for everyone — a strategy that you can change. Be a catalyst for productive supervision where you work.

It is simple, don't boss — COACH.

The shepherd was there at the center of the chaos...

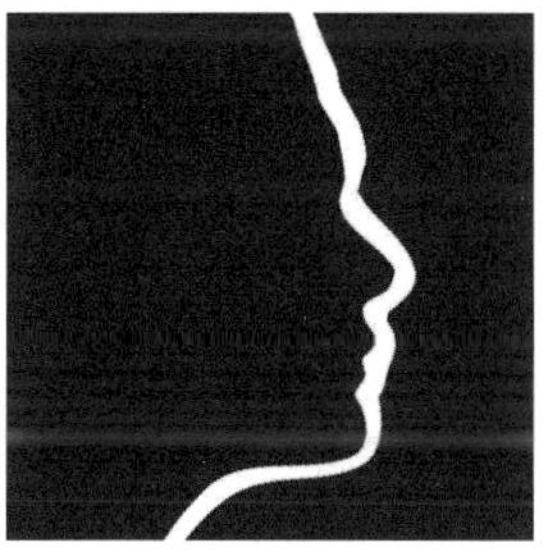

PETER:

smell a lot like the flock

Several years ago, I attended a high-level workshop on leadership. It was an intense complicated program, and by the third day of a weeklong course, I was thoroughly confused. At the coffee break, I confessed my confusion to Peter, the course director. Peter told me, "Leadership is actually quite simple", and invited me to join him on a short afternoon walk. As we strolled across a broad field, he told me a story about a walk he had taken as a young man when he sought to better understand the essence of leadership.

I was walking across a field toward the crest of a hill. As I reached the hilltop, I heard a distant racket and began to sense the smell of animals. When I reached the crest and could see a large valley below, it was clear that the noise and smell belonged to an enormous flock of sheep. From my perspective at the top of the hill, the flock moved purposefully across the wide valley.

For some reason, I was compelled to take a closer look. I worked my way down the hillside into the flock. As I became engulfed within, I was shocked by the chaos of the flock. From within, all I could sense was din and random movement.

The dichotomy of perspectives suddenly hit me. From the crest of the hill, the flock was clearly directed and purposeful, but at its center the flock was chaos.

Then I saw him — the shepherd. He was right in the middle of the chaos, nurturing a panicked lamb separated from its mother, nudging a young ram determined to move against the current, calming a ewe frantically searching for her lamb.

I noticed something important about that shepherd:

He was not at the front of the flock waving a flag.

He was not at the rear of the flock brandishing a cattle prod.

No, the shepherd was there in the center of the chaos, nurturing, nudging, calming.

*And it became crystal clear — this is the essence of leadership.**

That short walk with Peter and that simple story cleared my confusion, and the details of the leadership workshop began to fall into place. As we walked back into the conference center, Peter said,

"Forrest, one more thing

— the most effective shepherds

smell a lot like the flock!"

***Peter J. Neary, Leadership at the Peak, Center for Creative Leadership, 1995**

You will do things your way more enthusiastically.

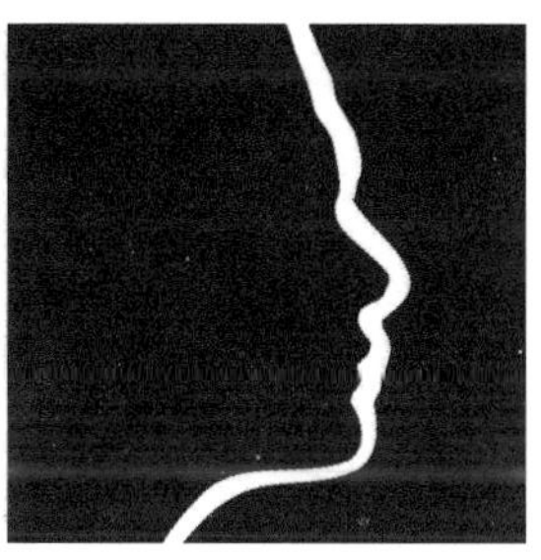

BILL:

the 80/15/5 rule

When I first started working in the pharmaceutical industry, my company had a Research Director named Bill that I respected greatly. Somehow, even though he had a rigorous schedule, his door was always open. He seemed to always be aware of everyone's work.

One day I went to his office and said, "Bill, you obviously know the goals of my research and you keep abreast of my progress, but you never question my approach or techniques. Shouldn't you, as Research Director, be questioning me more?" He responded, "Forrest, this is your work. You are the expert. You are closest to the details. I am confident that if you conduct the research your way we have the highest probability of success. If you run into a dead end, come in and we will discuss your options in dealing with the problem."

Several months later, I went to Bill's office. I had been struggling with a technical problem for weeks and finally thought that I had turned the corner on its solution. I said, "Bill, you obviously could see that I was really challenged by this project, and yet you let me twist in the wind. Couldn't you have saved a lot of time by helping me solve the problem?" Bill responded immediately, "Forrest, this is your work. You are dedicated to it. Perhaps I could have intervened with a solution, but you learned so much by trying different approaches that will be productive for us in the future — your way was better."

About six months after that, Bill unexpectedly called me to his office. He came immediately to the point, "Forrest, I noticed in your status report that you are taking a course of action that I know is unproductive and unprofitable for the organization. I want you to alter your approach. Let's discuss some alternatives." I was more than surprised, and said, "Bill, you always encourage me to do things my own way — Why change now?" Bill said without hesitation, "Forrest, about **80%** of the time your approach is best because you are the closest to the work and will do things your way with more enthusiasm. We both profit and so does the company. About **15%** of the time, I might know a more efficient approach than you, but you will do things your way more enthusiastically. We both benefit and so does the company. But, 5% of the time, I know your approach will be disastrous. You will be harmed professionally, I will be less effective managerially, and the company will not profit. This situation is in that 5%."

Years later I got the opportunity to take on managerial responsibilities. I followed Bill's 80/15/5 Rule for supervision and delegation. I discovered an extra benefit that he had not shared with me. By concentrating on that critical 5% and leaving people alone to manage the remaining 95%, not only were they more motivated and productive, but I had a great deal more time to be creative and productive myself.

You have to act like a man to get ahead.

YOU'VE COME A LONG WAY BABY, MAYBE:

what we can do about the glass ceiling

Not long ago, a colleague faxed me an article she had read in a weekly magazine. She said that the story, depicting the many barriers that a female physician had to overcome in order to attain the position and salary for which she was qualified in a well known hospital, was a familiar one to most professional women, including herself. I was greatly frustrated by the overt gender discrimination described in the article, but even more so by the lack of responsibility exhibited by the male leadership of the hospital to help develop the careers of women in the organization. For some time, I have been curious about statistics indicating that, although women have made gains in employment, very few reach the highest levels of management, and most do not reach the positions or income that they

The barriers that remain hurt us all, women and men alike.

desire. Many have called this phenomenon, which relates to the assembly line as much as it does to the board room, as the Glass Ceiling.

I have worked with many organizations dedicated to women's health issues, so I am naturally interested in women's workplace experiences. I therefore asked several colleagues, most of them women, to join me over a lunch of pizza and soda to discuss this Glass Ceiling. The women who joined in our discussion were from most functional areas and various levels of the company. They described the Glass Ceiling to me through very personal perspectives.

One woman said, "We can get to some point in organizations, but can't get higher." Another noted, "Women can see opportunities, but they are not accessible." Most agreed with one who said, "Women don't get equal pay for equal work." Clearly, in the last generation, women had to break down barriers just to get into the doors of our institutions. Clearly, progress has been made, and women are now playing greater roles. Today, many women occupy visible leadership positions, but the barriers that remain hurt us all, women and men alike.

We talked about causes of the Glass Ceiling, and it seems that "subtle things keep women from moving up" within organizational structures. Some of these relate to the idea that "organizations are built on male models" of career behavior. "You have to act like a man to get ahead." "Women manage differently from men," "Men don't like women as supervisors" were three explanations. However, another set of issues centered on the value that is placed on families — "organizations are not receptive to the needs of women and families." One said, "Only women have to choose between career and family." Another said that often "Women self-select less demanding career paths," because of family responsibilities. A third stated, "You have to give up everything else to succeed." Another noted that "It is usually the woman who has to leave her job to follow the man in a career move."

Most agreed that "80% of the housework and family responsibilities is done by women," and that "housework is undervalued" by society. They also recognized very pragmatic factors that influence women's access to top organizational slots. "In the context of a very competitive economic environment, people are afraid of losing whatever job they have." "Women (and men) are working 80 hours a week to succeed." They also stressed that this phenomenon does not only affect white collar women in upper level positions, but applies to all women such as factory workers who can't get beyond a certain level. Women who are marginalized, such as those in minority groups, are especially affected. They described the Glass Ceiling as whatever keeps women from attaining the achievements to which they aspire.

I wanted their insights on ways that I (and other men and women) might address some of these issues. I would like to share this insight.

Men, in roles as leaders, colleagues, husbands, partners and fathers can act every day to break the Glass Ceiling. Women, in roles as leaders, colleagues, wives, partners and mothers can also act every day —and encourage the men in their lives—to break the Glass Ceiling.

Read the list that follows, check off every strategy you can—and will—act on and start making change today.

As a leader:

- ❑ **Examine organizational policies and practices for their impact on women and families.** Make sure that women and men have equal opportunities for growth within the organization. Look at workloads, schedules, equal pay for equal work, attendance at conferences and management courses, job sharing, telecommuting, childcare, children at the workplace, dress codes. Regardless of your level in the organization, ask whether there is an egalitarian environment. If you are in a position to change policies and practices — change them.

- ❑ **Model family-friendly behaviors.** Are you an icon of workaholism or do you project a more holistic image that reflects the importance of family and community? Take parent leave. Bring your children to work from time to time. Take them to the doctor's appointment. Go to the school meeting.

- ❑ **Place women in leadership positions.** Seek women for Boards of Directors and all levels of management and government. Establish women role models for other women in the workplace.

- ❑ **Place men in support positions.** Seek and hire men to fill entry positions and for jobs traditionally held by women. Guide them in valuing women as leaders.

- ❑ **Don't tolerate negative male or female stereotypes.** Go beyond condemning sexual harassment. Foster women's assertiveness.

- ❑ **Facilitate positive professional behaviors in both women and men.** Select neutral topics (not just sports) for casual conversations between meetings that put men and women on equal footing. Involve women in decision-making. Celebrate that women have different views and management styles.

- ❑ **Value women's perspectives.** Delegate responsibility and authority to women. Develop leadership skills in women. Use language that is supportive and encouraging to women seeking professional growth. Mentor women and monitor their progress. Actively help them build credentials.

- ❑ **Turn your "Good Ol' Boy Club" into a "Good People Network."** Broaden your circle of advisors and colleagues to include more women. Encourage women to network with one another and with men. Make it easier for women to network with you as an organizational leader. Use your network to develop women's contacts, confidence and expertise.

- ❑ ____

  ____

  ____

As a colleague:

- ❑ **Examine your territory-protecting behaviors.** Ask yourself — do I really work as a team member?

- ❑ **Be willing to follow as well as lead.** Do your part to foster an equal environment for men and women. Contribute to the success of women who assume leadership positions.

- ❑ **Share in the housework of the workplace.** Pay your dues with the telephone answering, coffee making and cleaning up after meetings.

- ❑ ____

  ____

  ____

MEN—As a husband, partner and father:

- ❑ **Don't be threatened by your partner's accomplishments.** Her success doesn't diminish yours. Enjoy the benefits.

- ❑ **Support your partner's goals and work.** Give her time and encouragement. Expect her to succeed.

- ❑ **Value domestic work.** Acknowledge the contribution that it makes to your overall lifestyle.

- ❑ **Share in household responsibilities.** Don't have inflexible job designations.

- ❑ **Make parenting your personal priority.** Understand fatherhood as job-one. Actively involve yourself in lunch preparation, bedtime, taxi duty, etc.

- ❑ ____

  ____

As a parent:

- ❑ **Examine your attitudes about girl's and boy's roles.** Forget about "boy things" and "girls play with dolls." Play ball with both.

- ❑ **Develop your daughters and nurture your sons.** Guide girls to grow into strong women and boys to become gentle men. Have high expectations for both. Help girls and boys develop positive goals for becoming adults.

- ❑ **Be a positive example of responsible adulthood.**

- ❑ **Get a life.** Don't hide behind your "workload" or the "Channel Surfer." Grow with your family and do it for yourself.

- ❑ ____

  ____

  ____

I gained many potent insights that day, but I especially want to pass on a note that one young woman brought to me after our lunch discussion. She is a professional, a wife and a mother. She framed the Glass Ceiling in better perspective than I could ever do:

> *"To bring about a change of this magnitude would require a social change that needs to start at home and be continued and emphasized through the education system. Parents (both father and mother) must raise their children to learn to respect and support women, and to understand the importance of each member of the family in sharing responsibilities regardless of sex. I say children and not only boys, because*

women are, in many instances, raised to accept the way society views and demands their roles to be. If this change happened, the product would be men and women competing at an equal level in life, having greater respect for each other, and making greater contributions in all aspects of their private and work lives."

I can only add that each of us, but especially men, are empowered to act as agents of such change. So I call on each man to take actions every day to break the Glass Ceiling. Each man has the power to positively influence his organization, his coworkers, his wife or partner, and his daughters and sons, so that women can have greater opportunity to grow, achieve and contribute.

I believe that every man who will take such actions will vastly improve his own career, health, and lifestyle. Obviously, to take the above actions men will have to better integrate all of their relationships in the workplace, family and community. I firmly believe that each man who invests in such a holistic role will earn great dividends.

If they can't see where you are going, you must go where they are seeing.

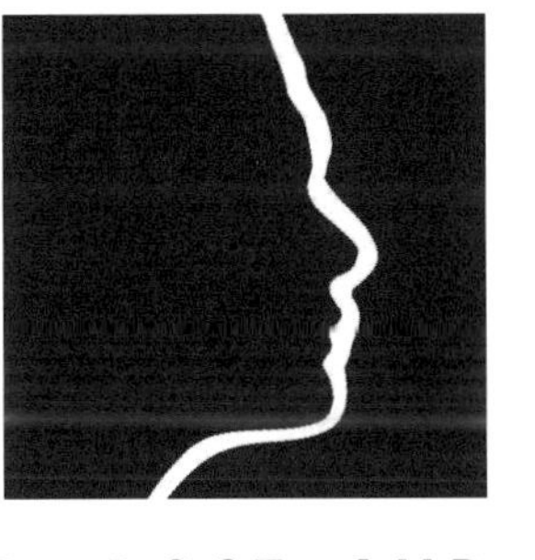

NED, ROSE AND ME:

near-life experiences

Have you read Betty Eadie's book, "Embraced by the Light?" Eadie writes about people who have survived near-death experiences, and the incredible impact these experiences have on their future lives. Well, I want to talk about a kind of experience that has even more impact. I call these near-life experiences.

What do I mean by near-life experiences? We all have them sometime in our lives. A near-life experience is a critical decision point — an opportunity to live the life you want. A near-life experience is an opportunity to take that first step on a pathway leading to a more productive, influential and satisfying life.

Unfortunately, too many people don't survive their near-life experiences. They don't take that step. They don't seize that opportunity. Something inside them dies. We all know people who have not survived their near-life experiences. At best, they are the middle-aged men and women who are hanging on until retirement so they can do the things they have always wanted to do — to "really live." At worst, they are the people who in desperation harm themselves or their coworkers. How sad! Too many people live lives never experiencing life to its fullest.

There are thousands of reasons for not surviving a near-life experience — fear of the unknown, family responsibilities, economic uncertainty, inadequate self-awareness, poor self-confidence and on and on.

I am going to tell you three personal survival stories. These are stories about people who faced critical life decisions, and made life-enhancing choices. These are stories about people who survived their near-life experiences.

Ned

My first near-life survival story is about Ned, a friend and former business partner. Back in the early 80's, Ned was caught in a corporate down sizing. After 18 years of employment, with a major pharmaceutical company he was without a job with only a few weeks of "parachute." I was working in New York City at another company, and I asked Ned to serve as a consultant while he made a career transition. We spent many lunch hours walking around Manhattan's eastside, figuring out Ned's professional alternatives. We examined all of the things that big corporations have to offer.

- Job security did not have much value — Ned had just been let go after 18 years.
- Fringe benefits did not have much value — we calculated that the average "fringie" package added up to about $2500 per year.
- Growth opportunities, job satisfaction, and feeling of accomplishment all seemed pretty elusive at the time.

One day Ned said, "For two cents, I'd start my own business." When we looked at things really objectively, there wasn't much keeping us tied to "corporate America."

The next day something amazing happened. An opportunity presented itself as a call from an executive search specialist. He was looking for someone to design and oversee the worldwide introduction of a contraceptive for an international non-profit organization. Guess who immediately came to mind — Ned and me!

The non-profit could not pay me the salary that I was getting in the commercial sector, nor could they provide me with the stock options that I was receiving. But armed with the insight from my walks with Ned, I negotiated a part-time position, with time to start our own business.

Ned and I ran that business together for nearly ten years, until I moved to take over another company. Ned refocused the business and grew it beyond my wildest expectations.

Back in 1982, Ned and I took that first step. Ned stayed on that path. Ned now controls his own life and finances. Ned works on the things that he holds most important. Ned is flourishing. Ned survived his near-life experience.

Rose

My second near-life survival story is about Rose, a woman that I met about one month after I had joined the New York based non-profit organization. I walked into the coffee room one day, and sat down with Rose and another female colleague that I already knew. I immediately noticed their "long faces" and subdued demeanors. I asked what made them so down hearted. Rose said, " There are no professional opportunities." She explained that she was there as a short-term post-doctoral appointment. Her husband had not yet relocated from California. Then Rose said, "There are no jobs anywhere for me." I asked her why she believed that. She replied, "I am a demographer and there are only four jobs for demographers in the entire world." I thought for a moment. Rose was doing what so many of us do — she was defining herself in the "box" of her education. I said, "Rose, I don't see a demographer; I see a bright young professional with a complex array of interests, talents and experiences, including your educational experience."

I invited Rose to my office and offered, "If you take one hour and do an exercise with me, I guarantee that you will find a satisfying productive career opportunity." Rose looked skeptical, but joined me. I simply started Rose on a networking process. I picked five colleagues' names from my Rolodex file in order to make phone introductions for Rose. These were people in quite diverse occupations, but who shared Rose's interest in math. I asked Rose not to define herself as a demographer, but to discuss her interests and experiences. I also asked her to request from each contact the names of five additional people that she might contact.

Well, Rose landed a job in the pharmaceutical industry doing statistical analyses of clinical research. After a few years, another company hired her to direct an entire department. When I last heard from her, Rose was thriving. Rose no longer defines herself too narrowly. Rose is aware of the breadth of her potential. Rose is open to life's opportunities. Rose survived her near-life experience.

Me

The third near-life survival story that I want to tell you is my own. Several years ago, I became President of a not-for-profit company. What I did not know when I accepted the position, was that the Board of Directors had been at war for some time. In fact, there was a small Board faction that was opposed to my hiring. A key person in that faction just happened to be the Chairperson of the Personnel Committee, the group responsible for my yearly performance evaluations. After about a year, she approached me with a proposal to have the entire staff do a voluntary, anonymous evaluation of me. I like feedback and transparency, so I thought this was a good idea. I had been moving the organization along an ambitious strategic plan rather aggressively, and recognized that some staff members were beyond their comfort zones. We distributed evaluation forms and asked anyone who wished to participate to mail them anonymously to the Chairperson of the Personnel Committee.

Several months later, the Board and Staff came together for the organization's semiannual meeting. I was about three sentences into my President's Message to the entire group, when the personnel

Committee Chairperson interrupted my speech, attacking me directly. She later presented to the Board what she represented to be a report of the Staff's evaluation of my performance. The report stated, among many other charges that I had no vision, did little real work, did not understand the field, and was dismissive of the staff's emotional needs

Can you imagine how I felt? I was shocked! I was hurt! I couldn't believe my ears! How could I have been so blind to this perception of me? After several hours of grilling by the Board in private session, I sadly offered my resignation. I reasoned that if the Staff did not recognize me as their leader, I could not effectively lead the organization.

Late that night, I received a phone call from another Board member. She was in tears. She was extremely upset that I had resigned. She asked me to reconsider. She said that she did not believe that the report accurately reflected the views of the Staff, and that my resignation would be harmful to the organization. After some further discussion with the entire Board, I agreed to stay on for six months to a year and evaluate whether I was the best leader for the organization. The Chairperson of the Personnel Committee resigned from the Board.

This was the most difficult year of my life. Can you sense how I felt? Day after day I stood, wounded and bleeding, before my staff, working to rebuild a productive relationship and to execute the strategic plan we had committed ourselves to accomplish.

Well, the healing process took time, but was successful. As a matter of fact, on my watch, the organization's income increased five-fold, sales of our medical products increased nearly three-fold, and the manufacturing process gained an international quality certification.

But this is not the important part of my near-life experience. During the reconciliation process, I attended a leadership program for CEOs and other high level managers. This was a weeklong total immersion experience of self-exploration directed toward improving leadership capacity. We underwent extensive evaluation and feedback, including that from our own employees, colleagues and supervisors. At the end of the program, I met with the faculty member who had observed me and had collected data on my activities all week. She led me through

If they can't see where you are going, you must go where they are seeing

the volumes of information generated in the evaluations and exercises. She summarized my strengths, weaknesses and priorities for self-improvement.

She told me something that changed my life forever. She said, "Forrest, you are a very intimidating person." I was confused! I view myself as a rather quiet and unassuming guy, certainly not intimidating. She explained, "Forrest, you have unusually long-range vision and you are unusually organized and determined to achieve that vision. You move people toward that vision with unusual vigor. This scares people to death."

Then she said something that crystallized in my brain, "Forrest, if they can't see where you are going, you must go where they are seeing." "If they can't see where you are going, you must go where they are seeing" She continued that the single most important thing that I could do to improve my leadership capacity was simply to improve my ability to communicate to people in their own contexts.

I came back from that experience determined to improve my communication skills. I refocused my personal mission and redefined my own strategic plan. I now view that the most important priority in my life is to communicate the simple management lessons that I have learned to future leaders. I now have a strategy for gaining the skills that I need to accomplish that goal. I now have the comfort with myself to stand before people from all walks of life and tell my story. I am thriving! I survived my near-life experience.

Now, every story should have a moral and I will try to give you the moral of mine. It is very simple. Some day, you will come to that fork in the road that will be your near-life experience. You will have the opportunity to take that first step— to be your own missionary — to live your own values — to find your own voice. Or, you just might succumb to one of the thousands of reasons that people find to live life without experiencing life to its fullest.

Please, prepare your self for this day. Be ready.

Survive your near-life experience.

Embraced by the light, Betty J. Eadie, 1994

...deep springs where our fundamental values and interconnections flow freely and clearly.

REFLECTIONS FROM THE FROG POND:

a personal glimpse of common ground

The psychologist and philosopher, William James said at the turn of the last century, "I know that you, ladies and gentlemen, have a philosophy, each and all of you, and that the most interesting and important thing about you is the way in which it determines the **perspective** in your several worlds."

Perspective — What is perspective? For me, it is very simple — perspective is what I see from where I stand. It is my special view from my special vantage-point. Each of us has special experiences that are the focal points of our lives — some cataclysmic (like a war), some seemingly trivial. I want to share one small personal experience that remains at the center of my perspective — my view of things.

As long as I live I won't forget my first visit to the frog pond! Just a kid of 10 or 12 perhaps, I was seldom indoors. No, my natural habitat was the woods and creek beds that edged our little town in upstate New York, extended by intermittent visits to the nature section of the school library.

My niche included the rabbits, blue jays, monarch butterflies, giant tree fungi, fossils and minnows that I stalked each day and read about every evening.

Then I discovered the frog pond. It was nothing of note at first; just an old muddy pool on an abandoned farm, where cows had likely drunk in better times. I was attracted by the growing ends of cattails emerging from the previous year's drying and shredded leaves at the interface of ground and cloudy water. It was about one foot from this edge that I saw the jelly-like mass that would frame my entire life.

There, gently undulating just beneath the pond's surface, warmed by mid-spring sunlight, was a clutch of frog eggs.

I returned to this spot each afternoon on my walk home from school, alone so as not to expose my precious discovery to the clods that I otherwise considered friends. They would not understand. They would stomp, and splash, and destroy, and laugh and leave. Alone, I observed for the first time that incredible segment of every life cycle called embryonic development.

I brought an old magnifying glass that my grandmother, who was nearly blind, used to see the Sunday funny papers. Through that bulging eye, I watched amazed as the randomly assorted eggs, white on one side and black on the other, rotated to position all of their black halves upwards capturing the sun's warmth. Over the next several weeks, I watched them divide and grow into spheres, elongate into rippling crescents, and ultimately hatch into swimming tadpoles.

I returned often to the pond to watch the tadpoles grow. Of course, each evening I read about amphibian embryonic development and natural history in the growing collection of overdue library books that accumulated in my small bedroom. This basic understanding about the connection of things presently living and things that will live in the future was the point of departure for my entire life's journey and passion. I read about reproduction and embryonic development of everything from primitive plants to human beings. At that time, my parents, teachers and friends often misunderstood my interest in human reproduction.

On subsequent trips to the pond I watched the tadpoles metamorphose into frogs, resorbing their tails and growing legs.

I also began to understand another set of delicate interrelations, those involving the changing embryo/tadpole/frog and the changing environment in which it lives. My evening reading began to include books on conservation and the environment.

Looking back, my first glimpse of one of society's most vexing problems came from trying to extend my young boy's understanding of the developing frog embryo and its pond environment. I began to perceive mammalian embryos, including human embryos, in their environments. I began to perceive the complex set of interrelations between the emerging individuality of a developing human fetus and the individuality of a pregnant woman. I began to understand a dramatic tension between interdependence and autonomy of fetus and mother. I began to recognize the incredible responsibility that even this glimpse of human reproduction had placed on me. I am awed by this fundamental tension and the responsibility of any degree of understanding of it to this day.

It wasn't until I was a teenager that I heard about contraception. It wasn't until I was in college that I learned about abortion. It wasn't until graduate school that I became aware of population issues. I have worked most of my professional life in the turbulent vortex of women's reproductive health, population and environmental concerns. Even these controversial issues have always felt like sub-plots to the main mystery of emerging fetal life and maternal life that runs through my mind whenever the noise reduces to a level that I can hear myself think.

And when I can hear myself think this is what emerges:

People who have an abiding belief in the sanctity of life, and

. . . people who share fundamental beliefs in the rights of women, and

. . . people concerned about population issues, and

. . . people who care about our planet's environment

have a great deal in common.

There may be dynamic tensions at the intersections of these difficult issues. But there are also real opportunities for creative communion.

It seems to me that most issues confronting us today, and causing much of the chaos that stresses our lives, would be greatly diminished by a little communion.

I challenge each of you to seize every opportunity to find common ground.

I deeply believe that it is this common ground that will be the most fertile in which to nourish productive discussion about the most important and controversial issues of our time.

I return to that frog pond of my boyhood often in my mind, especially when the din of conflict rings loudest in my ears. And there,

. . . with the sun's low glint on muddy water,

. . . with iris shafts slowly responding to gentle surface ripples,

. . . with the trill of tree frogs, or chirps of leopard frogs, or croaks of bull frogs,

. . . I see common ground with precise clarity.

It also occurs to me that each of us must have such places; deep springs where our fundamental values and universal interconnections flow freely and clearly.

Where is my frog pond? ______________________________

____

____

____

____

____

____

____

____

____

____

____

It seems to me that in these times when harsh diatribe is screamed from the furthest pole on every issue, it is critically important for each of us to find our own frog ponds hidden somewhere in memory.

And, visit there often.

The only messages worth sending are on subjects in which you really believe.

FIND YOUR OWN VOICE:

*10 steps for orchestrating your own personal message**

The other day I ran across an old ragged paper back that I had bought in the ninth grade called "Satchmo — My Life in New Orleans." I remember my boyhood fascination with the story of Louis Armstrong growing up poor in that exciting city in those exciting times. It was the beginning of my lifelong love affair with jazz. Years later, my wife and I moved to New Orleans, while I attended graduate school. We had the great thrill of walking those very streets where Louis marched playing funeral dirges. We had the great pleasure of sitting in Preservation Hall, listening to the aging icons of

America's own music. Jazz musicians often speak of the experience of learning to communicate their unique musical message as "finding my own voice." I was thinking, "that's what I want to accomplish in management — I want to communicate my own message in my unique style."

Here are 10 steps I have learned that I know will help you orchestrate your own personal message:

1. **Break the ICE.** Remember, it is critical to introduce yourself to each person or group each time you interact.

2. **Convince others of your earnestness, sincerity and conviction.** To be in earnest is to convey your true feelings. Be natural but forceful. State your definite convictions.

3. **Organize yourself to communicate.** Your goal is to sell yourself and your own ideas. Organize your approach so that you make sense to other people in their terms.

4. **Show what you mean.** Use your body language to ensure that they receive the same message through their eyes as through their ears. A gesture is effective if it helps people understand your message. Express yourself.

5. **Try your voice.** Explore vocal variety to convey your sense of friendliness. Be natural, show your true personality. Express vitality. Show your force and strength. Paint shades of meaning with your voice.

6. **Work with your words.** Select precisely the right words required to communicate your ideas clearly, vividly and appropriately. Expand your vocabulary. ...Apply your skills.

7 **Choose subjects significant to your listeners.** Know how you want them to react. Do research. Know your facts. Organize your ideas.

8 **Phrase your appeal in terms of others' self-interest.** Make it persuasive. Convince your listeners that your interests coincide with theirs. Analyze their situations to choose your approach. Reveal your emotions.

9 **Expand your knowledge.** Select subjects appropriate to your interests. Research your subjects thoroughly, using resources relevant to you. Translate ideas and insights into your own words.

10 **Inspire people.** Challenge them to embrace noble motives or achieve their highest potential — but select subjects that have deep meaning to you. Organize the thoughts and beliefs you share with others. Seek common ground.

Is there anyone anywhere that doesn't immediately recognize Louis Armstrong's trumpet or voice? Is there any question about the sincerity of his musical message? To creatively communicate your own personal message it is also critical to speak from your own perspective and conviction and in your own style. The only messages worth sending are on subjects in which you really believe.

Find your own voice.

Adapted from Toastmasters International, Communication and leadership program, 1992

Three factors chill and solidify to produce formidable barriers.

BREAKING THE **ICE**:

how to thaw frozen communication

I recently met with a group of friends and colleagues who get together to improve our verbal communication skills. I posed a question, "What are the greatest barriers to communication?" I added that I was interested in communications in a broad sense, including person-to-person interactions, as well as public speaking.

Quite a few communication-blockers were offered:

- fear,
- poor understanding of information,
- poor listening,

- preoccupation with self,
- lack of respect for other's opinions,
- avoiding feed back on our ideas,

and a variety of emotions. When I attempted to summarize these and other factors that freeze communication, three words emerged:

Intimidation

Closed-mindedness

Evasiveness

These three factors, **ICE**, chill and solidify to produce formidable barriers to speaking, listening and thinking in more productive ways. I asked my colleagues to work in three groups for a brief exercise. Each group discussed ways to avoid one of the elements of ICE. After 10-15 minutes, one person from each group presented five actions that we can take to break through Intimidation, Closed-mindedness and Evasiveness. Here is their insight.

How to break the ICE.

Overcome INTIMIDATION:

Be direct — State clearly what you want the other person to understand or do.

Re-direct — Re-state opposing positions from your perspective and to your benefit.

Be friendly — Return even the chilliest reception with warmth.

Use humor — Disarm other's defenses with a laugh.

Be self-confident — You have nothing to fear but you know what!

Avoid CLOSED-MINDEDNESS:

Be kind — Your respect and concern for others will open minds.

Ask questions — Seek others' perspective and really listen to their views.

Mirror the other person — Sense what is important or what concerns others, and reflect you own interest and concern.

Find common bonds — Rather than focusing on polar positions, start with shared values.

Make friends — Friends open each other's minds more effectively than do foes.

Confront EVASIVENESS:

Take the initiative — You are the best person to express your point of view.

Be truthful — Facts are difficult to evade.

Stay focused — It is hard to evade a persistent point.

Practice active listening — Seek out what the person perceives and feels.

Be sincere — Your interest in two-way communication will induce trust.

The phrase "Breaking the ice" is used all the time to describe conquering the discomfort we experience with first interactions with strangers. I asked our group if anyone knew the origin of this phrase. One member said that it derived from icebreaker ships used to open frozen shipping channels. Icebreakers prepared the way for other ships and ensured open transportation. He noted that references to breaking the ice in relation to communication dates back to the 1600s.

We need this same help in preparing the way today, despite all of our advances in information technology. As a matter of fact, the way in which information (or misinformation) is transmitted globally in seconds makes it more important than ever to break the ICE. It is more important than ever to clear away Intimidation, Closed-mindedness and Evasiveness to ensure open communication.

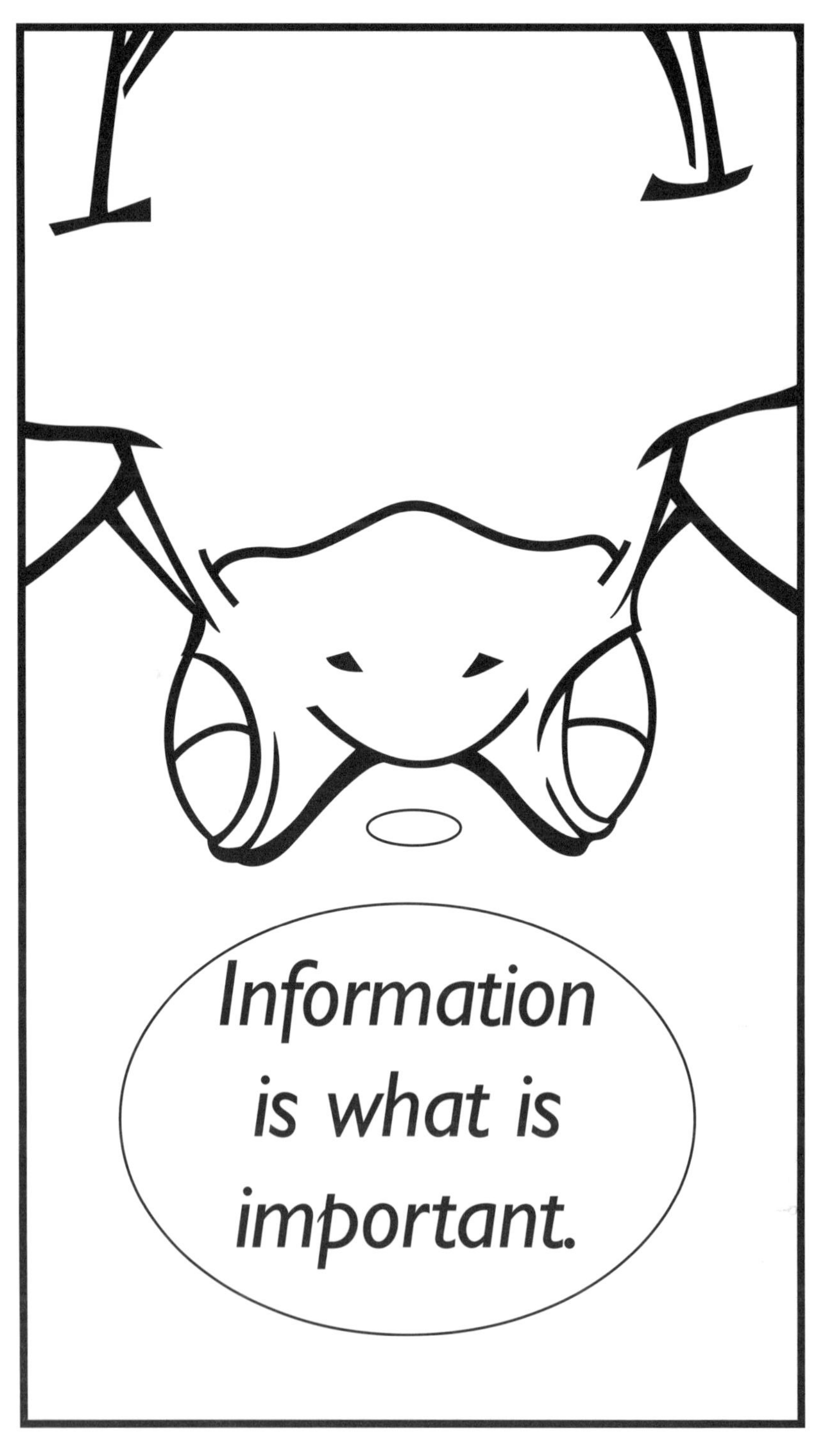
Information
is what is
important.

I.T. DON'T MEAN A THING IF IT AIN'T GOT THAT **SWING**:

think before you communicate

Information Technology — what an exciting world I. T. is producing for all of us! The Internet is making a global market place for goods and services. Intranets are allowing organizations to communicate internally as never before. Cell phones keep us constantly in touch. Virtual Reality allows us to experience places and situations that only yesterday were limited to our dreams. Of course, there are drawbacks to all technological innovations — including I.T. We are concerned about privacy issues, information overload, and the blurring of boundaries between our personal and professional lives.

I had an experience recently that highlighted such issues for me. We have all heard of email mistakes, big and small, that produced inconvenience, embarrassment, or catastrophic consequences. Ask Bill Gates about emails. I had placed an online bookstore on our website. I was excited to let friends and colleagues know about this venture, so I sent email messages containing hyperlinks to the bookstore internet address to professional groups with which I am affiliated. In general, the feedback that I received was very positive — phrases like "very creative", "entrepreneurial" and "a real resource." However, I was stunned to receive a stern email from the President of one group. He stated that I had made a serious breach of "netiquette" by using the club email list to broadcast a commercial message, and that I had jeopardized my relationships with other club members.

This obviously was not a life event, but it reminded me that no matter the technology (quill pen or Pentium chip), information is what is important. It reminded me that, while we exploit all available technologies to communicate, reaching people in their own contexts is what is critical. I have given a lot of thought to what is important to me in communicating information and perspective. My thoughts evolved into an acronym that I borrowed from that 1940's jazz composition, "It don't mean a thing if it ain't got that swing." I offer these thoughts to you to consider when you design that website, send that email or just sit down with pencil and paper. I.T. don't mean a thing, if it ain't got that **SWING.**

So — What is SWING?

Substance
— the subject matter of thought, discourse or study; the actual matter of a thing as opposed to the appearance; the meaning or gist.

Concentrate on the essence of your communication. Do research. Get the facts right about your subject and understand its significance to your audience. Address the basis, meaning, and import of the issue. Provide your understanding of its reality.

Wording
— the manner of expressing or phrasing.

Think about your phraseology. Take time to express your point of view in your parlance and style.

Integrity

— soundness of and adherence to moral principle and character; the state of being whole, entire, or undiminished.

Approach the subject with honesty and uprightness. Deal with it in its entirety. Show the soundness of your information and arguments.

Nuance

— subtle shades of color, expression, meaning and feeling.

Share your understanding of the subtleties of the issue. Be sensitive to shades of meaning. Share your suspicions concerning causes of problems. Offer your hints about solutions.

Grace

— elegance or beauty of form, manner, motion and act; pleasing or attractive quality or endeavor.

Review what you have written or designed before it "goes out." Does it reflect the elegance, polish and refinement that you want people to associate with you? Does it communicate humanity, compassion, benevolence, and courtesy?

We truly live in revolutionary times. The Information Technology revolution will markedly change every facet of our future lives. But, some things do endure. The need for human communication is older than humanity itself. The same instincts that prompted primitive drawings on cave walls will manifest themselves in some as yet to be conceived virtual reality. But please remember — Technology will never be more than the vehicle for that communication. Please remember — I.T. don't mean a thing if it ain't got that SWING.

Oh! One more thing.

SWING makes better verbal communication too.

Don't bother starting unless you are prepared to commit the entire organization to an all-consuming process.

MANAGING IN CHAOTIC TIMES:

how to grow a more decisive organization

"We need to be able to trust that something as simple as a clear core of values and vision, kept in motion through continuing dialogue, can lead to order."

From Margaret J. Wheatley's Leadership and the New Science: Learning About Organizations from an Orderly Universe, 1992

Growing more decisive management structures in today's chaotic environments is the most daunting task facing leaders at all levels of governmental, civil and commercial organizations.

Based on my own experiences in commercial and not-for-profit corporations, I offer ten thoughts on how you might grow a more decisive organization where you work.

1 **Don't bother starting unless you are prepared to commit the entire organization to an all-consuming process.** Having an expert in strategic planning sitting somewhere, even in the office next to the President, won't work. Even a strategic planning committee won't work. Every person in the organization will see this for the tokenism that it is. To even have a chance of success everyone, starting with the CEO and actively involving the folks on the production line, must be committed to a long-term process.

2 **Take a look backward.** You cannot decide where to go in the future without a real understanding of where you have been. Few organizations start this process de novo. Even start-ups have a past in the previous lives of their key stakeholders. Write an organizational history. Carefully examine the accomplishments, failures, traditions and culture of the organization's past.

3 **Ask every person in the organization four questions:**

1 Who are we?

2 What do we do?

3 How do we do it?

4 What do we believe?

The answers to these questions, taken together and projected into the future, form the best Mission Statement that an organization can script.

4 **Seed this Mission Statement** throughout the organization and use it as everyone's primary decision-making tool. Stress to each person that every decision, no matter how small, should be judged as to whether it serves to advance the mission.

5 **Explore individual values** that, taken in the aggregate, define the corporate culture. I want to emphasize the fourth

of the above questions — What do we believe? I think that it is crucial to invest the time and process to learn what is valuable in the work and work environment to people at all levels. This will make stakeholders of people who otherwise would only be employees. From this process you want to be able to craft the following sentence, "This organization's mission is anchored in the belief that —", and have most people in the organization feel authorship of the statement. By the way, the vision and values of the CEO, top management, and the Board of Directors are critical focal points of this process.

6 **Define the principles and practices** that guide the organization, based on the values exercises. These constitute your internal environment.

7 **Take an objective look** at your organization's strengths and weaknesses. Don't delude yourself. An organization's weaknesses may well present its greatest opportunities for productive change. Also look outside your organization to the opportunities and challenges that you must confront. This is your external environment.

8 **Define initiatives that will pursue the mission,** growing from strengths, strengthening weaknesses, while remaining true to the values that underpin the organization. Keep the list of initiatives small and focused. Be confident in the your organization's advantages. These initiatives will define the needed institutional capacities, the products and services that are your competitive advantage and will manifest your mission. They also define the changes in structure and management function needed.

9 **Consider stakeholders outside the organization as potential clients, capable of furthering your mission.** Whether they are investors, funders, collaborators or competitors, they are potential customers of your products and services. Other organizations, and key individuals in them, are as important resources as those in your own. Sell them on

your mission and understand theirs. Learn their strengths and weakness. Search for common values and goals. Negotiate alliances that support your mission.

10 **Collect data on performance,** feed it back to all levels, ensure improvement, and start all over again. There are numerous cycles in every organization's life. Annually, goals must be defined and monitored, budgets must be set and met. In my experience, the strategic decision-making process works best on an approximately three-year cycle. Assessing the progress made in accomplishing the initiatives, rethinking the mission, probing values, and articulating new initiatives, capacities, and needed organizational development will produce a continuously self-informing and constantly decisive organization.

"Cycles are the heartbeats of understanding. A thing perceived is just an event. Repeated it opens up to the instruments of science, the ruminations of philosophers, the imaginations of shamans."

From Tyler Volk's Metapatterns:
Across Time, Space and Mind, 1995

There is no more important leadership intervention to the long-term health of our institutions.

PASSING THE **TORCH**:

thoughts on responsible leadership transfer

I recently retired from the Presidency of an international not-for-profit corporation. For some time, therefore, I have been thinking about the importance of responsible leadership transfer in growing a healthy decisive organization. I believe that the Board of Directors and Staff of my former company managed the transfer of leadership through an exemplary process, the principles of which are valuable to decision-makers in most organizations.

Whether you are the Chairperson of the BOD, the CEO, Director of a major functional group, or technical leader in a project team, you will have to transfer your responsibilities to a new leader many times in your career. Whether you hold a leadership position in your workplace, place of worship, or community, you will need to manage the impact of leadership change on the health of that organization at some point. There is no more important leadership intervention to the long-term health of our institutions than responsibly transferring that leadership.

Here are five simple principles for passing the TORCH:

Transparency
— the quality of being easily seen through or detected; obvious

This is the most important and the most difficult principle to follow. Transparency is critical because nothing produces anxiety throughout an organization more than uncertainty about the person at the helm. Transparency is difficult because it requires those people in charge to share their own uncertainties about future leadership of the organization. It is critical at the earliest possible time to disclose to virtually everyone in the organization:

- that a leadership change is planned;
- why the change is needed;
- the time frame anticipated; and
- the process to manage the leadership transition.

Organization
— a structure through which individuals cooperate systematically to conduct business

Like any critical element of management, leadership transfer requires significant human and financial resources. This must be recognized as the priority for the successful accomplishment of the organization's strategic plan. Analyze the qualities of leadership needed to execute the future initiatives of the plan. Dedicate key individuals within and outside the organization to advise and direct the process of identifying, attracting and hiring the most appropriate new leader.

Responsibility
— being able to be trusted or depended upon; reliable

The outgoing leader must never leave a significant void for his or her successor. A successful transition plan must include a process of downloading the outgoing leader's understanding of organizational history, vision, mission, culture and managerial mechanisms to other members of the leadership team. This will involve a certain level of discomfort for all involved. The outgoing leader must delegate more and more authority and decision-making, while the remaining members of the management team must take on more and more responsibility. The goal is to have a completely reliable management team for the new leader, whether that person is selected from within the organization or from another. If the outgoing leader is not truly a "lame duck" by the time the succeeding leader is chosen, he or she has not done a good job of leadership transfer.

Communication
— The exchange of thoughts, messages, or information, as by speech, signals, writing, or behavior

As important as transparency is within the organization, communication to outside stakeholders is imperative. Uncertainty outside the organization about the person at the helm is as dangerous as internal anxiety. Investors, partners, collaborators, customers, and other influential individuals should be informed of the planned leadership change. They need to be assured of the organization's long-term health and direction. They should be engaged in the search for a new leader.

Harmony
— agreement in feeling or opinion; accord: a pleasing combination of elements in a whole

No matter what reasons prompt change at the

top, leadership transition is a great organizational opportunity. If planned and managed properly, such transitions can serve as catalysts for re-evaluation and agreement on re-vitalized vision and mission. The process can bring about broader conformity to updated strategy and management. The circumstances of working together to execute transition can energize an atmosphere of cooperation and generate new rapport within and outside the organization.

Passages are always challenging, no matter how well they are planned and managed. There are always daunting issues to be addressed by outgoing leaders, succeeding leaders and individuals who facilitate orderly succession. The simple principles that I have suggested in this essay can guide the leadership transition process, and make such passages easier; these simple principles can make passing the TORCH a tool to improve your organization's health.

Passing the TORCH is a tool to improve your organization's health.

An organization is healthy only if it is composed of healthy individuals.

TAKE GOOD CARE OF YOUR **SELF**:

vital signs of healthy organizations

I began this book with the fundamental premise of the Simple-Minded Manager. People are selfish. They are motivated by their own self-interests. Each person simply accomplishes the most when his or her individual self-interest is being served.

If you read a lot about management and organization development, you also see a great deal about organizational self. The discussions around organizational self are not overt, but we are constantly urged to make our organizations:

self-actualizing

self-adjusting

self-directing

self-evaluating

self-interpreting

self-inventing

self-maintaining

self-motivating

self-policing

self-scrutinizing

self searching

self-sustaining

—and the list goes on and on and on.

So, what is an organization's self? A dictionary definition of self is "complete individuality, nature or character" — probably as applicable to organizations as it is to individuals. But I have a different concept of organizational SELF, a set of organizational vital signs that monitor essential organizational health.

This is organizational SELF

Serve
— This relates primarily to an organization's Board of Directors.

What does it mean when you say, "I serve on a Board?" I'm not talking about hiring, firing and fiscal responsibility. What does it really mean to serve? The word serve has the following connotations:

- to act as a servant
- to wait on
- to render assistance
- to be of use
- to do duty.

Look at these synonyms for "serve."

- attend

- benefit
- minister
- advance.

If you are a member of a BOD, ask yourself — How well do I **Serve** the organization and its people?

Execute — This is primarily related to the CEO, the Chief Executive Officer.

What does it mean to execute?

- to carry out fully
- to put completely into effect
- to do what is required
- to give force to
- to give validity to
- to put to death (There are times when a project or a product must be terminated for the health of the organization).

Synonyms for execute include:

- perform
- achieve
- fulfill
- govern.

If you are the CEO of an organization, ask yourself — How well do I **Execute** the mission, values, policies, principles and initiatives of this organization?

Lead

— This is primarily important to the management team. Lead means:

- to guide on a way, especially by going in advance
- to set a course or direction
- to bring to a conclusion
- to go through, as to lead an exemplary life.

Synonyms include:

- guide
- conduct
- direct
- escort, shepherd
- pilot, show, steer.

If you are on the management team, ask yourself — How well do I **Lead** both the Board and the Staff?

Follow

— This is critical to everyone in the organization. I want to dispel any negative feelings that you might have about the idea of following. "Follow" means:

- to come after in sequence, order or time, as in a proud tradition
- to accept as a guide, such as mission, values or corporate culture

- to act in accordance with, as a set of principles

- to keep up with and understand, as the events that impact on the organization.

Synonyms are:

- ensue

- succeed

- engage, pursue

- proceed

- to attend or **serve**!!!!!!

I think that it is interesting that we have come full circle, in that we are back to the word "serve." And so, I ask each person in every organization to ask yourself — How well do I Follow the mission, values, goals and initiatives of this organization?

I ask each person in every organization to check these organizational vital signs:
BOD: How well do I Serve? **CEO:** How well do I Execute?
Management: How well do I Lead? **Everyone:** How well do I Follow?

For a healthy organization:

Take good care of yourself — an organization is healthy only if it is composed of healthy individuals.

Take good care of each other — an organization is healthy only if it truly senses its aggregate identity.

Take good care of your SELF — Serve, Execute, Lead and Follow.

It's not easy being simple-minded!

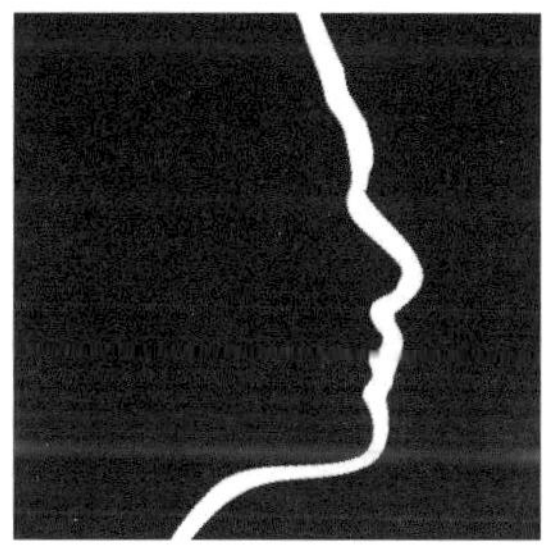

THAT'S WHY THEY CALL IT WORK:

a final thought

In these essays, I use acronyms and the meaning of words a lot to frame the lessons that I have learned. The simple explanation is — I did this to make them easy to remember. But there is a more important reason. Words are powerful dictators of behavior. I have learned the importance of choosing words carefully. Once words are out of your mouth, on paper or out on the Internet, you can't get them back. By looking carefully at the various meanings and connotations of the words we use, we are better able to understand and articulate clear, yes simple-minded, explanations in the most complex and chaotic of circumstances. This often requires considerable thought, time and effort.

It's not easy being Simple-Minded!

Do you have Simple-Minded Management lessons to share?

Dr. Greenslade would love to learn from you—email him at greensladef@intercare21st.com.

Pay us a visit online at: http://www.intercare21st.com.

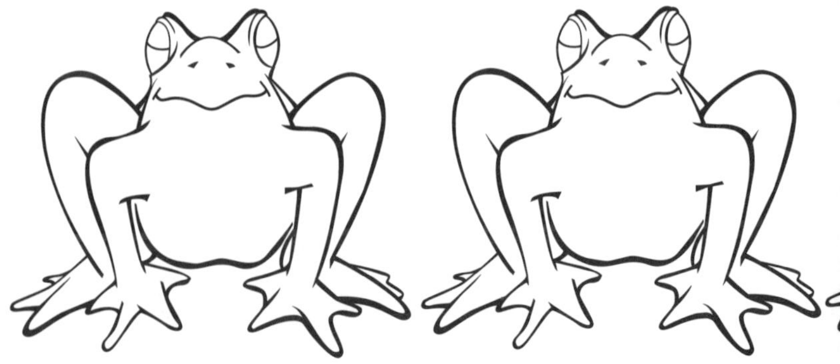

Five fat frogs
are sitting on a log.
Four decide to jump off.
How many frogs are left?

Turn the page.

Five...deciding and doing are very different things!

Order Form

I want to order a copy of

The SIMPLE-MINDED Manager

Cutting Through Your Work-Life Chaos

by Forrest C. Greenslade, Ph.D.

Name: ______________________________

Position: ______________________________

Institution: ______________________________

Mailing Address: ______________________________

____

____

Phone: ______________ Fax: ______________

Email Address: ______________________________

I have:

☐ Enclosed a check made payable to BookMasters, Inc

☐ Included my credit card number:

Card number: ______________________________

Card exploration Date: ______________________________

Signature: ______________________________

Price: $19.95 + $4.00 S/H; Non US orders + $10.00S/H

Please fax this order form to: 419-589-4040

Please send it via U.S. Mail to: P.O. Box 338, Ashland, OH 44805

You may order by phone at 800-247-6553

You may order direct online at: www.intercare21st.com.

Please note: You may want to photocopy this page and keep the original in the book!

How can I help you become Simple-Minded?